PREPARE AND PAINT YOUR BACKGROUND

Scandinavian painted furniture draws on the rich, deep colours popular in that part of Europe during the Baroque period of the late seventeenth century.

Preparation can be minimal. Make sure surfaces are clean and non-greasy. Gloss finishes – paint or varnish – need sanding back with medium-grade sandpaper to provide a 'key' for the paint. No need to fill cracks and surface blemishes; these add character to a rustic painted piece. The sturdy stool and pine cabinet were both painted using standard matt emulsion paints, intermixed for colour variations. Emulsion is the modern decorator's choice because it drys fast, is easy to apply, and provides an excellent surface for decoration. In this case, it also imitates the 'dry' texture of traditional home-made paints based on ingredients like buttermilk, egg yolk, fruit juice or berries, and seaweed.

TO GIVE EXTRA DEPTH OF COLOUR THE RED SURFACES OF THE STOOL WERE PAINTED WITH RUSTY RED MATT EMULSION OVER A WARM CREAM EMULSION. WHEN DRY THE TOP COAT WAS RUBBED BACK WITH MEDIUM-GRADE SANDPAPER – OR DAMPENED WET-AND-DRY PAPER – TO GIVE GLIMPSES OF THE PALER COLOUR BENEATH. THE BLUE SURFACES HAVE BEEN VERY LIGHTLY DISTRESSED IN THE SAME WAY.

DEEP EARTHY SHADES LIKE THE ONES USED HERE TRANSFORM A SIMPLE RUSTIC LAUNDRY BASKET INTO SOMETHING QUITE SPECIAL. BOLDNESS BOTH IN COLOUR AND IN DESIGN IS EVERYTHING WITH THE FOLK STYLE OF PAINTED FURNITURE DECORATION. EXPERIMENT WITH DIFFERENT COLOUR VARIATIONS UNTIL YOU FIND ONE THAT SUITS YOUR DECOR.

THE HEARTY COLOURS OF

Scandinavian rural painters used colour to counteract the tedium of winter darkness, so that the interiors of wooden cabins were often as vivid as flower gardens. Softwood furniture was invariably painted to add colour and excitement against a background of dusky wooden plank and log walls. A warm, blood red is still a favourite colour in Nordic countries, used for clothes and embroideries, as well as in furniture decoration. It is

OLD SCANDINAVIA

usually balanced with the deep blue-green used here as the base colour on the sturdy, homely pieces of furniture in this Scandinavian-style cottage. Look for chunky items of furniture to paint with the Scandinavian patterns.

Panels like the ones on the settle and the small cupboard are ideal for folk motifs. Keeping to the same base colour throughout is a good way of linking together disparate items from different periods.

PAINTING WITH A PATTERN

Start with simple motifs in a few colours – none of the patterns used here is difficult to paint.

Shown here are the steps involved in tracing off and painting the daisy border and yellow heart motif which give so much character to the simple wooden stool.

Points to remember: ● Use a hard lead pencil for the tracing down because this will give you a clear outline. ● Keep a clean copy of the tracing patterns – you might like to photocopy them a few times. You can then cut them up to fit awkward spaces without worrying about losing the originals. ● If you cut smaller pieces of transfer paper, be careful to leave yourself a big enough piece for the largest

TRACING DOWN AND FILLING IN

Repeating patterns are easy to apply and always look convincing in this style of rustic decoration.

1 FIX PATTERN IN PLACE WITH MASKING TAPE. SLIP TRANSFER PAPER BENEATH.

2 WITH SHARP PENCIL TRACE OFF MAIN OUTLINES OF DAISY PATTERN.

3 USING MEDIUM BRUSH AND COLOUR A, DAB IN DAISY PETALS, ONE STROKE TO EACH PETAL, WITHOUT TRYING TO MAKE THEM TOO REGULAR.

4 BOLD RED (COLOUR B) AND FINER BRUSH ARE USED TO PAINT LINKING LEAF SHAPES AND DAISY CENTRES.

motif. ● All the patterns in this book were painted with fast-drying artist's acrylic colours, available in tubes from all artist's suppliers. These dry with a matt finish, and are used thinned with a little water to 'single cream' consistency. Use an old plate as a palette. ● Use soft watercolour brushes in different sizes to paint motifs, including one fine one for outlining. There is no need to buy expensive sable brushes – synthetic bristles or mixed hair are fine.

MATERIALS CHECKLIST

WELL-SHARPENED HARD LEAD PENCIL, SCISSORS, MASKING TAPE, OLD PLATE, WATER JAR, KITCHEN PAPER OR TISSUES FOR WIPING BRUSHES, RULER OR TAPE FOR POSITIONING MOTIFS.

ACRYLIC COLOURS IN ULTRAMARINE BLUE, COBALT, RAW UMBER, WHITE, CADMIUM RED AND CHROME YELLOW.

THREE WATERCOLOUR BRUSHES, ONE FINE, ONE MEDIUM, ONE LARGE.

COLOUR RECIPES: (A) WHITE WITH TOUCH OF RAW UMBER

(B) CADMIUM RED WITH TOUCH OF RAW UMBER

(C) COLOUR A WITH TOUCH OF CHROME YELLOW

5 WHEN PAINTING A LIGHTER COLOUR SUCH AS THE YELLOW (COLOUR C) OVER A DARK COLOUR LIKE THIS RED, IT IS A GOOD IDEA TO PAINT IN THE MOTIF FIRST WITH A LIGHT OR WHITE UNDERCOAT. THIS WILL MAKE YOUR COLOURS FRESH AND GLOWING.

EXUBERANT CLASSICAL MOTIFS ARE

Many traditional motifs from the Rococo period were built up with swirling, curving brush strokes. Practise these on spare paper until they flow confidently.

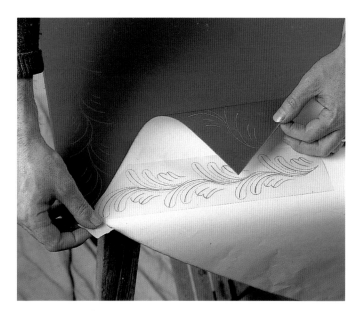

1 SECTION OF ROCOCO BORDER TAPED TO THE SURFACE, PRIOR TO TRACING OFF. RATHER THAN DRAW AROUND EACH LEAF, SIMPLY DRAW IN CENTRAL 'VEIN'. THIS SAVES TIME AND CREATES SPONTANEITY.

2 USE COLOUR A AND LARGE BRUSH TO FILL IN ELONGATED TEARDROP SHAPES. NOTE TRACING IS MINIMAL ON LEAVES AND BRUSH IS BEING USED TO BLOCK IN SHAPES.

1 USE MEDIUM BRUSH, WELL LOADED WITH COLOUR C, TO MAKE REGULAR DOTS AND FLOWER SHAPES. A GENTLE PRESSURE IS ALL THAT IS NEEDED. COLOUR D FORMS CENTRE.

COLOUR RECIPES

(A) 2 PARTS ULTRAMARINE BLUE, 2 PARTS WHITE, 1 PART COBALT, 1 PART RAW UMBER

(B) ULTRAMARINE BLUE WITH TOUCH OF RAW UMBER

(C) WHITE WITH TOUCH OF RAW UMBER

(D) CADMIUM RED WITH TOUCH OF RAW UMBER

Paintability

●

THIS PAPER PROTECTS
THE BLUE TRACING PAPER

●

IVEN THE FOLK TREATMENT

3 USE CLEAN LARGE BRUSH AND COLOUR B TO ADD
DARKER 'TADPOLE' SHAPES.

4 USE MEDIUM BRUSH AND COLOUR C TO 'DRY BRUSH'
HIGHLIGHTS OVER PALE BLUE SHAPES. PICK UP COLOUR
ON BRUSH, THEN RUB MOST OF IT OFF ON KITCHEN PAPER
BEFORE STARTING. TEST BRUSH ON SHEET OF PAPER FIRST.
THERE SHOULD BE JUST ENOUGH COLOUR TO LEAVE A
CLOUDY LINE.

1 FAT SCROLL SHAPES, ADDED TOGETHER, CREATE A
CHARACTERISTIC MOTIF IN SCANDINAVIAN PAINTED
DECORATION. NOTE HOW SCROLL SHAPES ARE SIMPLY
TRACED OFF AS LINES.

2 'DRY BRUSH' TECHNIQUE IS USED TO DRAMATISE THE
MOTIF BLOCKED IN WITH COLOUR A. COLOUR B CREATES
A SHADOW. 'DRY BRUSHING' WITH C DRAGS ON HIGHLIGHTS.

AUTHOR'S TIP Supporting your brush hand with your other hand helps to steady
your brush. This makes all the difference in achieving steady, controlled brush strokes, especially in the
middle of a large painted area.

1 BRUSH IN ALL TRACE-DOWN SHAPES WITH COLOUR A AND MEDIUM BRUSH. THESE INCLUDE LEAVES, 'TADPOLES' AND DOTS.

4 USE COLOUR C AND LARGE BRUSH TO 'WHISK' IN PLU 'TADPOLE' SHAPES ON VASE AND CENTRAL LEAF SHA

COLOUR RECIPES

(A) 2 PARTS ULTRAMARINE BLUE, 2 PARTS WHITE, 1 PART COBALT, 1 PART RAW UMBER

(B) ULTRAMARINE BLUE WITH TOUCH OF RAW UMBER

(C) WHITE WITH TOUCH OF RAW UMBER

By now you are beginning to feel relaxed and confident with your brushwork. A different approach is being used here for the floral set piece in our Scandinavian painting pattern. The same three shades of dark blue, light blue and off white are used to create a vigorous panel-filler, showing stylised flowers and leaves in a classical-type urn.

2 COLOUR B IS USED WITH A CLEAN MEDIUM BRUSH TO FATTEN UP THE DESIGN AS SHOWN AND SUGGEST STRONG SHADING AROUND MAIN SHAPES.

3 COLOUR C AND A FINE BRUSH PICK OUT DETAILS, HIGHLIGHTS AND FLOURISHES THAT ADD GREATLY TO THE CHARM OF SCANDINAVIAN DESIGN.

5 THE CLOSE-UP SHOWS HOW EFFECTIVE SMALL 'FLICKS' OF WHITE (COLOUR C) ARE IN ADDING LIVELINESS AND RICHNESS TO A FOLK DESIGN.

6 TO FILL A LONG ELONGATED SPACE, THE WHOLE BOUQUET MOTIF CAN BE REVERSED AND TRACED OFF JUST BELOW THE FIRST, CREATING THE EFFECTS SHOWN.

AUTHOR'S TIPS
Norwegian 'Rosmaling' painters stress that it is much harder to paint the left-hand side of a symmetrical shape. If this is your problem, try turning the piece around.

A STARRY INTERIOR

Play around with your pattern elements before deciding which looks best where.

A rich mix of motifs on the same piece gives this stocky little cabinet a peculiarly Scandinavian charm. Many old Norwegian cupboards were decorated inside as a background to the family's prized pewter, china or linen.

THE ARTLESS DAISY DRESSES UP THE SIMPLEST WOODEN COAT OR CUP RACK. THE SAME DAISY MOTIF MAKES AN APPEALING DECORATION AROUND THE TOP OF A QUAINTLY RUSTIC TABLE WITH A BASE MADE OF JOINED-UP TWIGS. THE SCROLL SHAPES MAKE A HIGHLY DECORATIVE FRAME FOR THE DATE PAINTED IN THE MIDDLE OF THE TABLE. FOLK PAINTERS LOVED ADDING PERSONAL TOUCHES LIKE THESE. A SET OF INITIALS WAS ANOTHER COMMON CHOICE.

FOLK PATTERNS AS BRIGHT AS THESE INVARIABLY LOOK BEST ON A DISTRESSED BACKGROUND COLOUR. HERE THE DARK BLUE-GREEN EMULSION PAINT HAS BEEN RUBBED BACK FIERCELY ON THE OUTER EDGES OF DRAWERS AND DOORS TO REVEAL THE WOOD. TO SOFTEN THE BASE COLOUR FURTHER THE WHOLE PIECE WAS THEN WASHED OVER WITH ULTRAMARINE BLUE HEAVILY DILUTED WITH WATER, THEN RUBBED OFF WITH A RAG HERE AND THERE. THIS GIVES A CERTAIN DEPTH TO THE COLOUR.

Splash colour about with both hands. It is no good trying to create a Scandinavian effect with timid half-measures or wishy-washy colour. Remember that these pieces provided all the colour in remote wooden cottages deep in snow; the colour needed to be brave and what Carl Larsson, Scandinavia's favourite artist, called 'hearty'. Inspire yourself with the colours of traditional costumes: scarlet, blue and yellow in brilliant juxtaposition.

SIMPLE SHAPES RESPOND BEST TO STRONG COLOUR SCHEMES. A TOUCH OF PAINTED DECORATION HELPS TO ENLIVEN THE RESULT.

POSITIVE COLOURS IN THE SCANDINAVIAN MANNER SET OFF A WONDERFUL JUMBLE OF TEXTURES IN THIS VIGNETTE FROM A WOODEN 'STUGA', OR COUNTRY CABIN.